ALL THAT WILL BE NEW

ALL THAT WILL BE NEW

Poems

Paul Mariani

ALL THAT WILL BE NEW
Poems

Copyright © 2022 Paul Mariani. All rights reserved. Except for brief quotations in critical publications or reviews, no part of this book may be reproduced in any manner without prior written permission from the publisher. Write: Permissions, Slant Books, P.O. Box 60295, Seattle, WA 98160.

Slant Books
P.O. Box 60295
Seattle, WA 98160

www.slantbooks.com

HARDCOVER ISBN: 978-1-63982-111-2
PAPERBACK ISBN: 978-1-63982-112-9
EBOOK ISBN: 978-1-63982-113-6

Cataloguing-in-Publication data:

Names: Mariani, Paul.

Title: All that will be new: poems / Paul Mariani.

Description: Seattle, WA: Slant Books, 2022.

Identifiers: ISBN 978-1-63982-112-9 (hardcover) | ISBN 978-1-63982-111-2 (paperback) | ISBN 978-1-63982-113-6 (ebook)

Subjects: LCSH: American poetry.

Classification: PS3563.A6543 A45 2022 (paperback) | PS3563.A6543 (ebook)

For Eileen, who made it all so possible. And so real.

Contents

Prologue: Northeaster at Prout's Neck | xi

I

First Light Last | 3
The Carpenter | 5
Poor Fauvette | 7
Wheat Field with Cypresses | 9
It Happens All the Time | 11
Huddie | 12
Elegy for Our 131-Year-Old Catalpa | 13
Instructions for Leaving Behind a Broken World | 15
Snow Moon over Singer Island | 16
The Poet as Eighty-Year-Old Sous-Chef | 17
One More Token of Beauty for the Taking | 18

II

Those Beloved Ghosts of Compiano | 23
A Sunday Afternoon on the Island of Grande Jatte | 26
Williams's Paterson Those Years Ago | 28
All That Will Be New in the World | 29
A Brief History of Cotton | 31
Harriet | 32
That Morning after the Assassination of Malcolm X | 33
Guernica | 36
On the Isonzo: Giuseppe Ungaretti, August 16th, 1916 | 38
One By One They Fall | 40

Covid Boogie | 41
Epiphany 2021 | 43
When Reality Hits | 45

III

A Periplum of Poets | 49
Remembering Phil Levine | 54
Separated by 2477 Miles, I Laugh with Bob Pack over the Phone | 56
Emily Waves from Her Bedroom Window as We Pass By | 58
The Other Side | 59
And Now | 60
The Call | 62
News That Stays News | 64
The Wheel, the Wheel. . . | 66
Supper at Emmaus | 67

Acknowledgments | 69

On this side it descends with power to end
one's memory of sin; and on the other,
it can restore recall of each good deed.

To one side, it is Lethe; on the other,
Eunoè; neither stream is efficacious
unless the other's waters have been tasted:

their savor is above all other sweetness.

—Dante, *Purgatorio* XXVIII. Translated by Allen Mandelbaum.

PROLOGUE: NORTHEASTER AT PROUT'S NECK

The primordial tensions of those natural forces.
Watch, as the massive waves surge forward, then back
out into the vast Atlantic, as if sucked into some blueblack
vortex, even as another wave and then another comes
crashing in to smash against the jagged granite shore.

The silver glitter spume explodes just feet away, as old
and now instant as that whirlwind confronting Job.
How is it Homer caught the drama in his *Northeaster,*
just yards from that rustic cabin there on Prout's
Neck along the coast of Maine back then? And now

the painting glowers in the cloister-like environs
of the New York Met, replete with a sleepy guard.
Homer caught it all. Schoolkids playing crack
the whip in those fields outside some one-room
schoolhouse. Those three Confederate prisoners

surrendering at Petersburg, to be interrogated by
a Union officer, one a hillbilly kid, another an old
man lost, and that young rebel officer, hand on hip,
his steady sullen staring in defiance even now.
Then, later, those Southern whites and blacks

in those unforgiving years of Reconstruction, that white
mistress standing awkwardly by the door, not knowing what
to say to her former slaves, nor they to her. Or those English
working classes, the Bermuda natives among the sands
and palmettos, the dangers of the sea, the drifting boat

with a lone black man as sharks circle him
with a typhoon rising in the distance. And in time
even people disappear from his canvasses, and it's
the sea alone the painter dwells on as at Creation's start.
As with the poet who must face the blank canvas

of the page and stare and stare and stare again.
And then, if he is blessed (or cursed) a word
at last comes uttering forth. And then another
and another. And then a line, a force, a tension
felt between a gray, a cobalt blue, a green, a dash

of red, an orange dot, and a smear of white to say
this is a painting. And then another swirl of white
as three waves spill, and then that giant wave
exploding, again, again, again, as the thing itself,
the real, comes crashing finally down on you.

I

FIRST LIGHT LAST

You arrive at enough certainty to be able to make your way,
but it is making it in darkness.
Don't expect faith to clear things up for you. It is trust, not certainty.
—Flannery O'Connor

And did you really think there would ever come a time
when things would go as you dreamed they should?
That you—you!—could hold the reins of some phaeton-
fated Seven Thirty Seven as first it whinnied then shrugged off
what you tried to make it do? You, you poor forked thing,
screaming as the plane bucked before it nosedived down
down and down into the unforgiving earth below?

Late January, Covid-killing time, and six below.
Sing it, pilgrim! Sputter those words out loud!
You're in the bughouse now. Oh, yeah!
You're in the bughouse now.

Remember that time, thirty years back, in those sea-
fungus-riddled-pitchblack tunnel mazes of Fort Adams?
How a woman tripped and fell just behind you
and you turned to help her up again, even as the guide
and those in front kept moving on, your wife among them,
as she slid into the dark and disappeared, like some Eurydice?

Remember (ha!) the blank fear you felt as you moved slowly
forward, leading the others nowhere, first turning right
then left, as you called out and the chambers echoed
their muffled sounds behind you and it hit you how you might
just be leading yourself and all those others into some instant hell,
some underworld, where the lost are trapped and will forever dwell.

Sing it, then, Homer, Hezekiah, Virgil. Sing!
Sing the desolation of those words. Go on! Sing!
You're in the bughouse now.
Oh yeah, sick seer, sad sod,
You're in the bughouse now.

Remember how you glimpsed that glimmer of light
somewhere up ahead, then slowly groped your way down
the tunnel toward it, only to come up against that
small grilled window, that *ignis fatuus,* that dead end
that had seemed to hold out hope, before it laughed
and mocked you? You, blind leader of the blind?

And then, in that darkness, in that mocking hell
hole of a maze, as those groans and curses swelled
around you, a light flickered and our guide appeared
and we followed her, this way then that, until we reappeared
once more, thank God, thank God, into the dizzle-dazzling
bluebell light, as the others, my Eurydice among them, cheered.

Sing it! Sing the sacred saving words,
again and then again and then again.
De profundis clamavi ad te Domine. . . .
Out of the depths I cry to thee, O Lord,
Pray for us, Mother, now and at the hour of our death.
Sing those praises from first light on into the night, and on,
until the blessèd dawn leads us home again.

THE CARPENTER

Georges de la Tour, *Joseph the Carpenter*, circa 1642.

Out of that darkness behind the man who turns
the augur into the wood which his left foot holds
steady, note how the light grows stronger

as it approaches the boy. Note too how the fingers
of the boy's left hand shield the flame of the candle
he holds in his right. From the creased brow and half-

glazed eyes you can see the man is tired. He's dressed
in drab like any other workman of the time, as on he works
into the night to put that daily bread upon the table.

Look again and see how alive the boy looks as he talks
to his father, trying to comfort him as the man keeps
on working. He's a handsome kid, dressed in a modest

red garment, so eager to share still one more story.
Then note how the candle flame, which alone illumines
the scene, seems to pass radiantly through the boy's

outstretched left hand, as if transfigured. How happy
the boy seems, his hand raised as if blessing the man
who raised him and who, except for giving the boy

his name, remains silent throughout Scripture.
Still, here in this night the boy seems to have all the time
in the world to spend with the man chosen to be

his protector, here in Nazareth, as in Bethlehem and Egypt,
though it's his heavenly Father the boy will call on,
beginning with those Temple elders when he turns twelve.

And the boy of course, being who he is, will seem puzzled
why his parents, who will search three days for him, don't
see why he must be about his Father's business.

But even that scene remains somewhere off in the distance,
and for now, note how the wood is being readied, like
the wood that will be waiting for him to complete his work.

By which time Joseph will no longer be there to watch over
his boy, though by then the hard lessons of patience
will have been drilled in: that readiness to say yes

to whatever task his Father has for him. How often
the story's been told, as here by someone who will see
his own family wiped out by a plague, along with himself.

Still, the story never grows old, does it? No matter how many
times you keep coming back to it—often in the dark—to see
how a man watched over a boy and the mother of that boy.

POOR FAUVETTE

Jules Bastien-Lepage, *Poor Fauvette*, 1881.

Late winter, and the little girl stares off, her gaze
reaching down into your soul. She's wrapped
herself in a makeshift shawl of brown cloth
to ward off the cold this very morning, as she stands
there in some wintry field out in Damvillers,
minding the family cow as it feeds on straw and thistle.

"There are some glorious pictures," D.H. Lawrence
wrote a friend, after viewing the canvas at a winter
exhibition some thirty years after Bastien-Lepage
painted the scene, the artist himself long since gone.
But nothing caught his eye like this scene, as he watched
the lovely woman in her smart, dark velvet suit

and hat, its feathers flowing down over her shoulders,
a woman so unlike that poor Fauvette. "Too sad,"
the woman whispered, as she confided to the man
beside her there. "But then that is what the country
does to one." And now, the moment over, the two
moved on to yet another landscape, and then another.

And here's the thing: it's the gaze of that little girl,
isn't it, that embeds itself upon your heart, before you too
find yourself likewise turning away. How many times
have you been stopped when you least expected
by someone asking you to look at them and listen?
Like the daughter of an old friend, himself long gone,

catching you in the frozen parking lot of the old brick
church just after Mass this morning, when all you
wanted was to climb inside your car for warmth,
her face and yours masked by this pandemic,
though her teary eyes spoke volumes as she began
to speak of the deep rifts between her brother and herself.

And what was there for you to do but listen in that
freezing morning. Pain is pain. Pain is personal. Still,
you've learned to listen, which somehow seems to help.
To help the other, as it helps your sorry self just to know
you care. Something that seems to repeat itself more
and more now, giving back something of yourself.

Like that bread just offered you, which you consumed
before you left the parking lot to head back home for
coffee, eggs, and toast. Which is more than what poor
Fauvette will feast on when she returns this evening
back home, cold and weary, to sup on her daily bread,
if that, both those gazes etched now on your heart.

WHEAT FIELD WITH CYPRESSES

Vincent Van Gogh, late June 1889.

"I have a canvas of cypresses with a few ears of wheat,"
Van Gogh writes his brother Theo back in Paris. There are
poppies in it, and a blue sky impastoed "like a multicolored
Scotch plaid." And below those mottled clouds beckons

that "wheat field in the sun," its rich thick yellow baking
in the dense summer heat. To the right are two tall
cypresses, reaching skyward to catch the eye's attention.
It's late July 1889, and Vincent's here at the mental

asylum in Saint-Rémy, suffering his dark night
of the soul. He's thirty-six and has just ten months left
to live before that bullet takes his life. In the time
he has, he will paint another dozen wheat fields

when the doctors let him walk about and paint
en plein air. And just now the wheat is ripe for harvest.
But it's those mottled paint-daubed clouds that catch
his eye, like those Father Hopkins, dead just three weeks

now at forty-four, caught sailing over Dublin the year before.
"Cloud-puffballs," he named them, as they glittered across
the skies. And once again you feel it: the wind, the Spirit,
as life springs once more back to life and dark gives way

to light. A farmer went out to sow his seed. Some
the birds ate. Some bleached and burned among
the brambles. And some fell on good soil, to produce
in time fields of golden wheat like this. Fresh winds

still shook the banks and brakes as spring came round,
Father Hopkins saw. And, look, once more birds
were busy building nests. Though just not him,
at least not now, what with sickness coming on.

And yet, both men got up again, again, and did what
they could with words or paint and soldiered on.
Whoever has ears to hear, let them hear, Christ urged,
as now another storm sweeps down the darkening fields.

IT HAPPENS ALL THE TIME

For Bruce Watson

As with the fluttering of the Firebird's wings, Nathalia
Arja in flaming red, regal, aloof, more birdlike than human,
the prince holding her in both arms, though he himself
seemed held captive by her presence. . . .

I thought of Jackson, that bearlike hound who lives
next door, rolling playfully on the lawn as we talked.
Then, in a flash, tearing after the unsuspecting robin
who had just come to rest under the flowering dogwood,

striking it so hard that it had only a moment
to flutter its wings before it lay still, its mate crying out
as it flew up into the branches of our copper beech,
his Eurydice gone now, ah yes, gone now forever.

It happens all the time, these tragedies. Kobe Bryant
and his sweet daughter Gianna now. One more flight
gone wrong. Or the young barber telling me how he lost
his mother in those twin towers twenty years ago.

Or my friend Bruce telling us that his brother was dead now,
a man who flew a million miles and more. All gone now,
unlike that Firebird who lives on in myth and hope,
fluttering her resilient arms as she rises once again.

HUDDIE

Our beloved English Springer Spaniel Huddie
was put to sleep this morning at eleven, down
in South Deerfield at the vet's. He was fourteen
years old and, until this past year, when the strokes
began to cripple him, had lived a good and gentle life.

Eleven years ago, when a well-to-do family whose son
was a student at Eaglebrook felt they could no longer
care for territorial Huddie, my son Mark stepped up
and adopted him. Hudson was the name they'd given him,
cavorting then on the Upper West Side overlooking

the majestic river which flows south into the Atlantic.
But whether Huddie himself ever understood the origins
of his name is a question no one has an answer for even
to this day. He went by many other names as well, bestowed
on him by our grandsons. Dweegin, Haysoi, Bobo,

even Sewer, this last for his lightning-quick ability
to vacuum down whatever you left unguarded
on the kitchen counter or on your plate or even
on your fork if you gave him the split second he
needed as he seemed to lie there sleeping at your feet.

And there he is now in those touching photos Karen took.
On long walks down country roads, or looking out at boaters
on some pond, or running through the golden autumn leaves.
Or carried by my son when at last his legs gave out, or on
the couch, cuddled by his boys, as if to say it was enough.

ELEGY FOR OUR 131-YEAR-OLD CATALPA

1889—2020

Our dear catalpa, whose angel-headed blossoms
flowered above us without fail each June for over
fifty years, our beloved silent guardian angel who
watched over this old house like the Lord's appointed
one, lies fallen now upon the harsh hard ground,
toppled with one fell swoop by some madcap
monster microburst that, truth be told, wreaked
havoc over home after home around the county.

Our neighbor, an arborist with a wicked sense
of humor, called the collapse of our *Catalpa speciosa*
a "wrenching loss," the tree being the largest of its kind
in western Massachusetts, and maybe the entire state.
Ah, how tall you stood, and proud, and revealed to so many
a sense of majesty and, yes, of quiet comfort, thou, home
to God knows how many woodpeckers, cardinals and jays,
not to mention bees, chipmunks, and those thieving squirrels.

You, the same proud form our old friend engraved in ink
with yours truly looking up into your leafy branches,
your overriding presence I wrote those poems about
when our boys were small, you, whom the arborists
came to visit as if on holy ground, standing tall in your
plot of pachysandra with a bit of poison ivy here
and there, beneath whose branches once stood our
bird feeder, too often ransacked by some cunning bear.

And in your shadow five well-cared-for boxes (one
crushed now), filled with tulips and bright daffodils
and amethyst astilbe. And just beyond: those purple
rhododendrons and burning bush and dogwood
planted thirty years ago when we lost our Sparky.
Changed, all changed, as now we await the men
who slab by slab will cart away your broken body.
Ah! But not those blossoming angelheaded memories.

INSTRUCTIONS FOR LEAVING BEHIND A BROKEN WORLD

Say it! Say it while there's time, even as your world
disappears, like that river crashing over the Great Falls.
Say it, the way Hardy or Williams would have said.

A teenage mother and a father (twenty-three) hurled
(or unfurled) together by destiny, Harriet's and Paul's.
Say what needs to be said, now that both of them are dead.

You keep telling yourself the story's over now, and done,
even as it keeps seeping back, morning, day, and night.
Random pieces of a puzzle with most of the jigsaw lost.

Try beginning with some "once-upon-a-time" begun.
That East Side tenement. The scalding water and the fright.
The looming shadows as they trapped you, and what that cost.

Summon up that first world for what it was: the hot tar floor,
you in your homemade Army outfit as your father walked down
the street to war, the bombers above the city that summer of '45.

Or your mother sewing pocketbooks for food for the four
of you, that orphanage you were sent to in the Bronx uptown,
your head smashing the windshield as Daddy braked. All that jive.

And on and on it goes, and no doubt will continue to do so
as long as there's a single breath to breathe. It will all be there
halfway through the night again, and there again come morning.

Listen up! It's time at last you left behind your nightmare status quo.
What's done is done. You have a family now to love. There's prayer.
There are still a few fast friends. Leave the dead to do the mourning.

SNOW MOON OVER SINGER ISLAND

Black velvet darkness, tufts of clouds heading slow-
ly up the beach, the February snow moon like the host
the priest raises shining now along the solemn coast,
transfiguring the Atlantic waters down below.

I sat there transfixed, as if for once at peace
with what I had the sense this time around
to see, the things that all my life have ground
me down at last drifting off to the east-northeast.

But what words can net what one feels in these too-brief
moments? Grasshopper transcendence, the poet called it,
those translucent wings whirring up into the Sunday light
before the shouts of strangers force their entry like some thief.

Show us a sign, we say, show us what we think we want to see.
Though do we even know what such a sign would be?
Or is the blessèd thing already there before us, you and me,
and all we really need to see it are the eyes to see?

THE POET AS EIGHTY-YEAR-OLD SOUS-CHEF

What better way to spend my time now than to play
the sous-chef as my dear wife prepares this very day
yet another of her heavenly meals? Cinnamon yellow
squash soup with hints of fresh mint, a melting mellow
eggplant Parmigian', chicken à la Française,
crumb apple pie. Ah, lucky me, to have been chosen
to dice the scallions and onions, peel the potatoes,
gather from our little garden parsley, basil, and some thyme,
then back inside to uncork a bottle of three-star wine.

Oh, to put aside the books that keep staring up at me
clamoring to be read: a fresh translation of the *Odyssey,*
Dante's *Convivio,* Flannery, Chesterton, and Joyce,
as well as a dozen poets, each with his or her distinctive voice
but who too often now remain unsung. And that pile of books,
each clamoring to be blurbed and praised, as by the looks
of it they no doubt deserve. But oh, that freedom just. . .to be.
But be what? And now it's half past five and she's calling up to me.
Time, dear, she sings, to be the sous-chef you were called to be.

ONE MORE TOKEN OF BEAUTY FOR THE TAKING

And God saw that it was good.

Just outside our kitchen window, in the shadow of
our eight-foot rhododendron, its leaves once more
furled in the January cold, the battered birdfeeder
stands atop its scarecrow pole, its scarred black baffle
long outsmarted by those four devil-may-care squirrels

who will not scare and so each morning take their sweet
time ransacking the rich mix of seeds meant for our
two cardinals, who at dawn and dusk will flicker, land,
partake, depart, and hopefully return. It's a feeder meant
as well for our six nuthatches, that pair of scolding jays,

those three mourning doves, four purple and five
gold finches, that bevy of sparrows, juncos, blackcapped
chickadees, and our solitary rat-a-tat pileated
woodpecker who comes and goes at the oddest times.
How do you put a price on visitations such as this,

as you fill a glass with water from the tap and your eyes
peer out? And yet, there they are, at dawn, mid-morning,
then afternoon and on into the winter evening's dusk. In rain
and snow and brilliant sunshine, these tokens of beauty
there for the taking, in their browns and blacks and whites,

with now and then a flash of reds and golds and dappled blues.
These gifts, these hints of Eden for the moment here restored,
unasked for but freely given, amidst the chatter of the same
old same old we call the morning news, even as that good
news blazes in on you through your kitchen window.

And beyond them the ghost of our catalpa, its ten-foot-wide hollowed trunk bleaching there among the heart-shaped snow-dusted pachysandra. And beyond that too those lilacs in the receding distance. And then the sky and stars, and all of God's creation, and all of it so good, so very good.

II

THOSE BELOVED GHOSTS OF COMPIANO

Wallace Stevens, late in life, evoking the ghost
of Coleridge, another poet philosopher, then
in his twenties, starting out on a packet bound
for Germany, invited by some Danes to share a drink.
He was dressed in black, with large shoes and worsted
stockings, so that they mistook him for some Methodist
on a mission, though the fact was he was on his way
to Göttingen to learn what language has to teach us.

"Doctor Teology?" they joked, half drunk and having
one hell of a time up on the deck. No, he said, no,
he wasn't that. Then what? "Un philosophe, perhaps?"
No, he said. That was the last thing he thought himself
as being, though that in fact was what he was.
Well, they laughed, weren't we all philosophers?
And with that he joined them for a song until all rose
"as one and danced on the deck a set of dances."

O happy day, when the philosopher and the poet
could sing and dance together, a cup of wine held high
in your hand, as angel-headed hipster Danes danced on
and the river flowed on and on beneath your feet
and evening descended gently with each passing moment. . . .
Each night now, as this plague keeps descending on us,
refusing to let go, my dreams turn strange and stranger,
as if I were some blind Orion searching for the rising sun.

Like you, I'm on a journey, though where I'm going
changes with each moment. Sometimes I'm in a car
driving with my wife beside me, who's there until she isn't.
Or I'm on a plane, every last seat empty now,
my destination unknown even to the pilot.
Or I'm on a boat, watching peasants dance
their madcap turns like the ones you see in Breughel's
Kermess, as some unheard music goes reeling on.

Mostly, though, I'm just walking, one step followed
by another. Sometimes there's a stranger walking
there beside me, but who never says a word.
And then—like that—there's no one there but me,
and I'm thinking to myself that if I just keep
moving on, I'll get to where I'm going.
The trouble is I don't seem to know where it is
I'm going, or even if there's any place to get to. . . .

When I was four, I remember walking with my father,
taking one giant step and then another to keep up.
We went bounding up First Avenue ten blocks to 61st,
one row of tenements after the other, till we came
to where he'd lived, though the building itself
had disappeared to make room for an exit off the bridge.
Old men he'd known with toothless grins sat on stools,
greeting us with that Val di Taro patois of theirs.

It was the spring of '44, and the Army
had finally called him up. And though some who'd
grown up with him would not survive the war,
he made it through, walking draftees through
the intricacies of carburetors and air-fuel induction.
And now here we were, my father come this one
last time for a glass of wine and to say his *ave
atque vale*. Hello, *compaesani*. And now goodbye.

Fifty years before, his parents sailed here to America,
where the streets they'd heard were paved with gold,
though the only paving my *nonno* ever knew
was the tar he laid, until the asbestos pulled him under.
Compiano was the town they'd hailed from. Giuseppe first,
then Giulia, who brought their firstborn with her. Primo,
run over at the entrance to this very Bridge the day after
Christmas 1907. He'd just turned twelve.

In time others in the family sank from history too, infants
mostly, what with cholera, pneumonia, and the rest.
Mary, with that large bow in her hair, made it to fifteen,
almost surviving the Spanish Flu before they lost her.
My father, who was three then, told me how he'd sat
there on her coffin, lost in the back of a horse-drawn
wagon, as they readied Mary for her final trip across
the 59th Street Bridge to Queens and Calvary.

I have walked the streets of Compiano twice now, once
with my own son Paul, and once with Allen, poet-
philosopher, who spoke in his polished Italian with the local
priest to learn what little could be gleaned of those belovèd
ghosts I know now only through a few inscriptions in the local
registry, much of the story, like so many others, burned
by German soldiers as they left the town behind them
in the spring of '45 and headed back across the mountains.

Still, what would I say to them, these beloved ghosts
of Compiano, if I should meet them? Or those others
who lie silent somewhere in my blood? What words,
poet-philosophe, would suffice? And still the river runs
beneath my feet as they sing on and on in dreams.
Is it that, in the end, there are no words? That there are
only ghosts now who keep calling out to us, beckoning us
to rise and dance along beside them while there's still time?

A SUNDAY AFTERNOON ON THE ISLAND OF LA GRANDE JATTE

Georges Seurat, *A Sunday Afternoon on the Island of La Grande Jatte*, 1884-86.

There they are, Parisians from the lower classes
mixing with the well-to-do, strolling about
the Isle La Grande Jatte as on the river flows.
It's a summer afternoon, the year 1884,
and the figures in the painting all seem
distant from the other, each one living
in the bubble of some private dream.

Still, they form a procession as in Phidias's bas
reliefs. "Modern people, in their essential traits,"
the artist said, all floating here, as if frozen
in eternity, coalescing in harmonies of endless dots.
Eight boats out on the river, forty-eight humans,
two dogs. Even a capuchin monkey in the foreground,
a favorite with Parisian ladies of the boudoir.

The painting was a scandal, one critic shouted,
observing the well-dressed gentleman strolling
cane in arm, replete with top hat and cigar,
the woman on his left in flowered hat
with purple parasol and dog and monkey,
the critic calling the couple for what they were.
In the left-hand corner there's an oarsman, puffing

on his long-stemmed pipe, oblivious to the couple
inches from him, the woman lost in her knitting,
the husband staring out into some vacant space.
Above them two young women, one fishing.
And beyond them, a soldier stands, playing his bugle
as if the park belonged to him and him alone,
the notes themselves hieroglyphs for us to read.

And there's a mother, a little girl in white beside her,
walking towards us while another runs off into the distance,
her stance frozen now forever. This was all pure Bedlam,
Critic Two observed, aware that the artist had crossed
some social line, where anyone it seemed could mingle.
It was all so crazy, growled Critic Three, made dizzy
by those thousand thousand dots of flashing paint.

Still, over and over the painter, who would die at thirty,
kept coming back to his summer's Sunday afternoon
there on the river as he morphed molecules of paint
into an Eden like nothing anyone had ever seen before.
And here we are, a century on, the question still unresolved.
How shall we read the scene now that everyone we see,
like the creator of it all, has left the stage forever?

WILLIAMS'S PATERSON THOSE YEARS AGO

Here is what I wanted to do, he said. Write about
the people close to me, to know them in detail,
the men and women and the kids playing
hopscotch and stickball on the streets of Passaic
and Garfield, Totowa and Clifton, Rutherford
and Paterson. Know the neighbors, know
the patients with their mumps and measles,
the nurses I worked alongside day-in day-
out, the police sergeant and the jailed drunk,
the mechanic in his grime-streaked coveralls
who ran the Esso station down the street,
the plumbers and carpenters and bricklayers,
the druggist over on Park Avenue for whom
I encoded messages on my prescriptions
which meant I didn't charge this patient so that
the druggist wouldn't either, the housewives
leading lives of quiet desperation along with the men,
the boys afloat tire tubes above the sewer main
by the grim-faced factories dotting the Passaic
in Wallingford, those immigrants from Naples
and Black families who'd made their way up from
Georgia, all picnicking now on the mintgreen grass
of Garrett Mountain those Sunday afternoons in May,
their language so fresh and raw it startled the way
cold water does when it splashes against your face.

Ah, that river of language, all these seventy years on,
recalling the graygreen river I too knew as a boy
when I zigzagged along the cliff above the Falls,
the river thundering as it crashed over then down
into the chasm below, majestic as always, despite
the scum of Styrofoam cups and condoms, the discarded
tires and dead dogs, everything swept up, then spilling,
carried by those spring freshets, as they still carry on,
haunting the ear of an old man who ponders the mystery
of it all, the re-verberating ever-vital river of language.

ALL THAT WILL BE NEW IN THE WORLD

will be anti-Puritan, Williams insisted, in one
of his best prose pieces, his admiration for Père
Sebastian Rasles spilling out as if confessing.
Larbaud the Frenchman began reading from a copy
of Cotton Mather's *Magnalia Christi Americana*

on the Mosaic-like manifest destiny of New England.
But Williams wouldn't have it. No, they were not
the ones to lead, those strong-willed Puritans
who saw only dark savages around them.
Better to learn from that Jesuit priest come down

from Quebec to live with his Abenakis, to eat their
dried seal and boiled wood if it came to that, and who
in the end would die with them. No, not Mather,
with his map in hand, but the man who stayed
in constant contact with his "*cher troupeau.*"

How Williams got it so right still moves me
all these years on. Unlike those who raged against
the natives, Rasles saw that "the head of logic"
must be relegated to its proper place, which was
in heaven, residing with the mystery of the *Logos*.

There was someone who could confirm what
a Jersey doctor, half Brit himself and half Puerto Rican,
someone who saw each day all of life and death
with its attendant sufferings. Someone who came
to see in all its scintillant beauty a new world naked.

Rasles too saw what the poet too must come to see.
That "every tree, every vein in every leaf" was part
of God's mysterious flower. That somehow it was
the "worldly flower of Rome whose perfume might
still draw all bees," even here in the mud of the Passaic.

How Williams came to despise the dry and splitting
logic that cut each flower from the glazed rain
water we all need to survive and flourish.
Both legs fractured as a youth, Rasles knew
what suffering was as he hobbled on with his people,

marveling the more as he learned their incandescent
words and ways. What warriors they were, with those
brilliant guerilla tactics they used against those bent
on robbing them of what was theirs with rum or
a strand of pretty red ribbon, or logic's words. . .or nothing.

Rasles knew in time the Englishmen would find and
kill him. Still, not even death would keep him from his flock.
Back in Boston, his bloody scalp garnered his killers
a hundred pounds. But you too know the places, don't you?
You who've lived here now for fifty years? Deerfield,

Hatfield, Hadley, the Abenaki and Pocumtuck names
long gone. Still, something lingers in the spray that tumbles
to this day at Turner's Falls, named for the one who killed
the Peskeompskut while they fished for salmon there, then
died himself, that sad history that lingers in the river's mist.

A BRIEF HISTORY OF COTTON

Cot, cotum, cottage, coten, coat, calico, cotton.
In the beginning the Arabs gave us *qutun*,
cotton grown in the Indus Valley for seven
thousand years, shackled like the word itself
to slaves, sold or bartered everywhere.
Seme di cotone, the oil from cottonseed, a favorite
of Italian nobles, *noblesse oblige.* Then came
the French with their *usines de coton,* then
the English, where cotton got mixed up wordwise
with flannel, if one can cotton that. Walloons crowding
into England brought their "fustians from Naples,"
linens mixed with India cotton, "a fruit of the earth
growing upon little bushes called Cotton Wooll."

And then there's America, pinchpenny
New Englanders with their looming factories,
weft and warp, their rumships and their slaves,
arm in arm with those gorgeous *Gone*
with the Wind plantations way down South
in Maryland, Mississippi, and Georgia, where Black
folk toiled from dawn to dusk year round, eating
what they could, sleeping where they could,
their children chattel, branded property of those
high masters who demanded a high return
on their investment. And so to cotton, meaning
a high nap on cloth, thanks to the field hands'
thankless work, a word meaning to succeed, rising
to a nap, meaning to get on well with, as opposed to
not cottoning to. Cotton: to get it, as if we understood.

HARRIET

Bruised feet brushing through falling leaves. The lingering bay of hounds off in the flickering distance.
Dark terror stabs her with each broken branch.
And one more field ahead where no birds sing.

How many times she turned back to fetch
another soul—body bruised, branded even—
from some cabin, signaling them to leave in
haste to head north on that freedom stretch.

They called her Moses, and they put a price
on her head. But nothing stopped her. Nothing did.
The whippings, the faces pocked and riddled with the horror of it, the maggots in the rice.

And that railroad running north and more north and
always she was there. There when Brown planned
his raid on Harpers Ferry. There as an army spy, or standing at the head on the Combahee Ferry expedition,

when she led out seven hundred sisters and brothers.
After the war she returned to Auburn to care for
her aging parents, founding a home for the sick and poor,
fighting for the near-invisible we call "the others."

God bless Arminta, Minty, child of Ben and Rit,
Mr. Thompson's property down by the Blackwater
there in Maryland, back in 1821 or '2 or. . . .
One of nine, three sisters sold off, as Massa saw fit.

Put forth once to adorn our $20 bill (she still might)
putting Andy Jackson (slave owner) on the back, where he
belongs. *White folks have been on these bills a long time, you see.*
Thus the powers to remind us how might makes right.

THAT MORNING AFTER THE ASSASSINATION OF MALCOLM X

"Terror on every side! Denounce him! Let us denounce him!"
All my friends are waiting for me to slip. They say,
"Perhaps he will be deceived; then we will prevail
over him and take our revenge on him."
—Jeremiah 20:10

"Get back on the train," he said. "Then go back
downtown to 59th, and take the Number One."
He was in his mid-fifties, I think, the man behind
the booth. Brown, soft spoken, eyes down.

"Then take the train back uptown to 116th
and get off at Columbia University." He told
me this, I have come to see, to keep me
from getting off the train there in Harlem

on that dead and silent morning. No, I told
myself. After all, I was already up at 116th.
Easier to just walk up the subway steps, cut through
the park at Morningside and on to the campus.

This was February 22nd, 1965,
a bright crisp Monday morning. I'd come up
on the subway from Hunter to get a copy
of *How to Read French* which the adjunct at Hunter

had assigned us. One more way of talking
I'd have to learn to pass my PhD exam come fall.
One more piece of that jagged jigsaw puzzle
I'd have to fit together if I was ever going to earn

my degree in English and Comp Lit from the dons
at the City University of New York.
Understand: I was a week shy of my twenty-fifth,
married now eighteen months, and living

in a two-family apartment on Booth Memorial
out in far-flung Flushing, our firstborn
already well on his way. The fact that a Black
man named Malcolm X had just been killed

with a blast from a hidden sawed-off shotgun
the afternoon before at the Audubon Ballroom
north of here in Harlem had registered, I think,
but barely. But what had any of this to do with me?

This was New York City, you have to understand,
and this was the Sixties. And what did I know
anyway about this Malcolm with that X in place of
some white slave master's name? And wasn't this

the guy who, when JFK was shot down in Dallas
fifteen months before, had said how the chickens
had finally come home to roost? The same man
who'd called Cassius Clay (now, thanks to him

Muhammad Ali) his close friend until they too
had parted ways (to Ali's too-late regret)? The man
who once took on William Buckley in that debate about
white privilege, and won? Only after I got my prized

degree and moved on to teach up in Amherst did I
begin to put the pieces of the puzzle back together
when I came at last to teach Malcolm's autobiography,
and learned what courage the man had to have to face

down the rank corruption in the leader he'd followed
for a dozen years, the prophet Elijah Muhammad,
and turned instead to Mecca for the strength
he saw the faithful offered so he could carry on,

in spite of being targeted by the FBI
and New York's Finest, the blind side of human
nature being what it is. Add to all of this his beloved
Betty there on that stage with him, mother of their

four daughters, with two more on the way, whom
he would never live to see. Add too the gunshot
wounds to his chest, left shoulder, arms and legs,
the blood gurgling from his mouth as he lay dying.

And hadn't the leader of the Nation, miffed at
Malcolm's leaving, made it known how the man
was now a traitor and so must die. And if he himself
washed his hands of the job, not so his followers.

And now Malcolm X Shabazz was dead.
Though not his message. No, not what he had
had to learn the hard way, about the cost of learning
to love your brother, black, brown, or even white.

That ice-cold morning, as I walked the ghostlike streets
of Harlem toward the looming Heights, two young
Black men in dark suits stood there on the sidewalk
talking, surprised to see a white man like myself

with a briefcase in his hand walking there, even as
it dawned on me that I might well be in the wrong
place at the wrong time. And here's the thing: like two
angels, they stared, winked, parted, and let me pass.

GUERNICA

Pablo Picasso, *Guernica*, 1937.

Like war itself, the painting will swallow you.
Eleven by twenty-five feet, a monster mosaic
made up of newsprint blacks, whites, and grays.
Welcome to the new normal with the blitzkrieg.

Cubist that he was, Picasso rendered the news
in unreadable fragments to mark that April
afternoon in 1937—Monday and a market day—
in the first city to be targeted by bomber aircraft,

which killed some sixteen hundred, mostly women
and children, while the men were off fighting
on the frontlines. How the spattered images knife
the message home to unveil the insane face of war.

On the left, below the drunk-eyed Minotaur-like bull,
let your own eyes fix upon that two-thousand-year-old
Pietà, a mother's head thrown back as she howls
the inconceivable loss of her dead baby. To the right

a gored horse, as in a bullfight all gone wrong,
the beast's scream, silent as it seems, echoing
the mother's cry. Then too the cries of three
other women, one wounded and dragging

her leg, one trapped inside a house as the flames
lick all about her. And another, a disembodied head
holding a lamp to keen the truth, unlike that electric
eye bulb that illuminates the Nada of it all.

At the base of the mural lies the mutilated body
of a soldier, eyes askew in death, one hand open
to whatever, the other still clenching a broken
sword, with a flower springing from it.

Note too the human skull somewhere in the mesh
of jumbled abstract screaming images, and the dove
midway between the bull and horse, perhaps a symbol
of the Holy Ghost, though it too cries out in anguish here.

Pilgrim, viewer, what shall we make of all of this?
German bombers over Poland two years later, then
England's cities. Then Dresden, Tokyo, Hiroshima,
and on and on as the the broken scroll of history unfolds.

ON THE ISONZO: GIUSEPPE UNGARETTI, AUGUST 16TH, 1916

I'm holding on for dear life to this mangled tree
left to lie here in this sinkhole like some circus
before or after the brouhaha erupts.
The clouds float quietly across the moon.

This morning I stretched out in an urn of water
and rested there like some relic. The river's currents
polish me like one of its smooth stones.

I pulled my bones together and went out
into the depths like some acrobat, then returned
to squat beside my uniform, filthy with war,
like some Bedouin bowing to receive the sun.

This is the Isonzo, where I have seen myself
at last, one more pliant fiber in the universe.

It hurts. It hurts to be out of harmony with things.
Still, hidden hands seem to immerse me here.
They grace me with a happiness I cannot explain.

These are the stages of my life, here in my rivers:

The Serchio, where for two thousand years my mother's
people and my father's have drawn their water.

The Nile, that saw me enter the world and begin to grow,
not yet understanding, there on those endless plains.

The Seine, where I came at last to know myself
among its quotidian currents swirling on and on and on.

These are my rivers, summed up here in the Isonzo.
These are my memories, where in each of my rivers
it comes home to me now that night has already fallen,
my life a blossom made up of shadows only.

ONE BY ONE THEY FALL

One by one they fall, the leaves, one by one.
The sugar maples first, then, by the back door
to the old garage, our red-berry-sour
kousa dogwood aflame in the setting sun.
And now those damson lilacs along the fence,
and, look, our new dawn redwood where our
catalpa all those years we've lived here stood.
And, yes, the cherry apples and the shad. . . .

Here, now, the furled leaves bid adieux
as they slip silently from the dappled branches
of our copper beech again, as if on cue,
dropping day and night one by one. Take
in their beige silk-crisp texture as each unlatches
and the rising wind twists them in mini avalanches
and rest among the hollyhocks. And hostas too.
Then think how in time those branches will shake

their way to bud and leaf again come spring.
Call it the silent language of our stalwart trees
that stay rooted there through drought and freez-
ing storms, signing their years with ring on ring.
Why is it that we find ourselves coming back and back
to them? What is it these gentle giants have to say?
Where would we be without them, our world lack-
ing leaves, like words gone silent as they lose their way.

COVID BOOGIE

Some guy swaggers into a supermarket without a mask
and a father, mask on with his little masked daughter
beside him, asks him to cover up or leave, as he oughta
to maintain some social distance, when suddenly the guy takes
a step away, pulls out a Glock from the back
of his belt, and points it at the father's head, then is heard to say
he don't like being threatened, so back off, Jack, OK?

An old woman—maskless—bumbles into some discount store
and a young woman employee—masked—rushes over
to explain that masks are store policy, and so needs to ask
her to obey the rules. She even offers the woman a free mask
while she's inside shopping, something for her own safety
as well as everyone's, even as customers go buzzing by
hunting for toilet paper and whatever else they're looking for.

But the old woman ain't having none of it. Says she has rights
too, guaranteed by Uncle Sam and the U.S.S. Constertution.
And to make her point, decides to plop herself down in the main
aisle until at last the manager himself comes over to explain
it's his duty to keep his customers safe. But no, she fights
stubbornly on, until finally she pushes herself up and wobbles her way
outside, middle finger up, then flings the mask by way of retribution.

August 2020. Three quarters of a million bikers, tattoo-
branded maskless bearded faces, descend once more on Sturgis,
South Dakota. And this being the real West, they mean to urge us
all to make America great again, the way it was, when Fort
Meade made its mark and Deadwood made another. Despite
the warnings of ten thousand doctors, though, here they are, hordes
of leather jackets, dungarees, and T-shirts reading "Screw

Covid, I went to Sturgis." Rebel flags, here, there, everywhere,
mixed with banners proclaiming "Don't tread on me" to make it clear.
And then there's guns and weed and topless chicks and beer,
adding up to brawls and crashes by the score, and more.
Masks, they sneer, are for dumb-ass liberals like me and you.
And didn't their main man Trump say this Covid thing's a flu?
Something he told us a shot of hydroxychloroquine would cure?

And on and on it goes, the wrecking numbers racking up each day
as now college kids like those I taught head back to school,
mixing Zoom and social distance classes, then head out to sway
to hip-hop strobe light gatherings at night as they share drool
and then they're tested and find they've caught it too (no way,
baby, this can't be!) and—like that—truth hits them between the eyes
and it's goodbye college, as all (or much of what) they hoped for dies.

Meanwhile ambulances wait in empty parking lots, one more stifled cough
echoing eerily by the ER entrance as drivers wait for the inevitable next call.
Think now, she said, think now of that *indescribable sorrow that follows
every lonely last breath when the ventilators at last turn off*.
Think too of our loved ones alone. Think of those final swallows
as the blue-lipped face turns up, the eyes, head fitted to a metal shawl.
Think of that mad captain dancing us down death's dark empty hall.

EPIPHANY 2021

From the days of John the Baptist, the kingdom of heaven has suffered violence.
And the violent take it by force.
—Matthew 11:12

After Herod's obsequious queries (the wizened geezer
on the brink of death himself) about where this
usurper king would spring up, the scribes searched
the scriptures and found the destined place a sheep town
five miles south of the city's walls. Herod bit his lip,
paused, smiled. *Find him,* he wheezed, urging the Magi on.

And let me know, so I too can pay this king you speak of
the homage he deserves (then, *sotto voce* with quivering
tongue and hissing mouth) *as I did with mine own sons,*
before I had them offed. And so the Magi packed their camels
and headed down to Bethlehem, King David's city,
though his line had seemed to die out centuries before.

Still, as the star once more led them, they came at last
to offer homage to a baby canopied in his mother's arms.
Gifts of gold and frankincense and myrrh.
Gold fit for a king, incense by way of worship,
myrrh to remind us of the end all are destined for.
But did they understand this was a new beginning,

like nothing even they had bargained for? Pray,
pilgrim. Pray for a word, a single note, like
that hungry jay outside by the feeder. Ask for the gift
of that single note dancing outward from within the other.
Three words would be enough. Three sillion-speckled words,
each dancing with the other to enflesh the living Word.

Cold, so cold. Storm clouds looming. Village streets deserted.
And three men searching for a star to guide them
to their journey's end, trying to discern, even as
one more power-hungry fool, clinging to his staff,
searches them for a way to breach and quench
that light to hold on to his sick, insidious designs.

Lord, help us to find that light in these dark nights.
This assault on those marble halls millions have walked
in peace and awe year after year. In Sylvestre's *Sack
of Rome* a Goth wraps his snakelike rope around the neck
of some statesman's statue to bring a sense of order crashing
down. Tell me, Lord, what are we witness to this time?

WHEN REALITY HITS

Strange utterances, horrible pronouncements,
accents of anger, words of suffering,
and voices shrill and faint.
—Dante, *Inferno* 3

Lord, how is it this Corona Covid nightmare
still chews up half the news night after night,
as exhausted doctors plead with us to stay
at home? How is it those beds in the makeshift
ICUs keep filling up and up and up
until exhausted nurses keel over with fatigue
or (worse) succumb themselves, and the numbers
of the dead multiply then rise and rise again?

Oh, dear God, please help us. Please save us
if it is your will. Or at least help us better
understand what this thing is really all about.
What is it you want us to take away from this,
as the coffins keep piling up in tents and makeshift
plywood corridors? We have read the sacred texts
and history books, searching the past and those plagues
of yesteryear for what they have to tell us now.

And still, *still,* here we are, a year and more into all
of this and, despite news of this vaccine and that
and, yes, of still more to come, with all those vials
swarming beelike off those cold steel counters
and those Fed-Ex trucks leaving docks and racing off
with police escorts somewhere to the rescue, though not
anywhere it seems near here. Still, we hold out hope
that light *(mehr licht!)* will come again. And soon.

But will it? And as the days and months roll on,
and one tenth of the promised number get their shots
and the news goes burbling on, we ponder what
the "new normal" will look like somewhere down the line.
Still, the restaurants stay closed, along with all
those gathering places—bars, gyms, even schools
and churches—and as we choke our words through masks,
we plead, dear Lord: what shall we take away from all of this?

III

A PERIPLUM OF POETS

Periplum, not as land looks on a map
But as sea bord seen by men sailing.
   —Ezra Pound, Canto 59

Then, turning from the dark, I saw a light come toward me.
And as it drew nearer I made out a face I knew I knew,
though the man had long since gone. Still, I could see

it was him. "Allen, dear friend," I said, "how good to see you,
here, now, even in this darkness. You, who brought light
to so many in your time. Your Dante, Ovid, your Virgil too,

among the voices your gift with words restored to life.
You above so many other guides showed me the way
to better understand my poets with their inner strife

and reconciliations flaring out before they settled on the page.
And here I am, trapped once again, these decades on,
the sands in my own hourglass nearly gone, dear sage,

and this the final journey to learn and lean upon
those poets I spent so many years searching for a reality
in those precious scraps they left, then as now drawn

to their words for what light they might offer me."
He nodded then to say he understood. Wasn't he here
now to guide me to those who'd helped me see? And be?

"Yes, I was your mentor," he smiled, "though it was clear
our paths would each go their way, and there would be a
time when another's words would call me here, you there,

me to Giudici and on to the Florentine's *Commedia*
and the one who sang of Rome, then Ovid's *Metamorphoses*
and my own *Chelmaxioms*. Call it a lifetime's encyclopedia,

as with Pound's shapeshifting cantos, so I might seize
the souls of genius for those coming after like yourself.
And you, *bubeleh*, nursed on the patois of Paterson, it seems

clear now how your own beloved poets filled your shelf
with the antagonistic cooperation that resonates and defines
you, gleaned from that Jersey doctor. Then too, that sense of self

discovered in the inscapes of your Jesuit, whose lines
captured the roll, the rise, the carol, the creation
of a world rising from blue bleak embers and shines

here, now, even in the dark, to lift the imagination
and offer you its consolation for the asking. Praise him,
praise this poet-priest restored to light, his heroic resignation

following his Master. It took thirty years to raise him
up and in time lead you through your own uncertain years."
"Not so fast," the one who let nothing ever phase him

interrupted. It was Huffy Henry, with his brilliant wit. But tears
too, for this bearded edgy man who suffered loss after loss
as he downed a whiskey then another and another, whose fears

of losing a father, two wives, and himself were there: the costs
of love and fame that led to lockdown and finally suicide.
"Call me the Lost Saint of Purgatory, who double-crossed

myself one too many times, and joked about it until the tide
went out and with it my clipped final Song, as I stared down
from that gelid bridge, having hit the booze again. And so I died,

waving adieux like my dear Hart, as I too hurled down, a noun
splitting from the words which give it meaning, to float
off into some abyss, and yet still hoping somehow to be found

again." "But in those *Addresses to the Lord*," I said, "you vote
for something more than Henry ever hoped for. How many times
you replayed Hamlet's play within a play, conniving to quote

those words to make Mother fess up to Daddy's death? The crimes!
The times! Still, in the end it was you there dead upon that floor
and not her or the man whose name you bore that rhymes

with *Bury Man,* as if all was foreordained. And now the long war
over." "Except," he said, "for my words which might still give
you and others hope." Then out of the dark a third shade, the raw-

nerved one who bled out his *Quaker Graveyard,* combative
as the bear he saw himself, a C.O. who refused to fight
for a country that bombed civilians. *That* he could not forgive

and so spent those months in jail, then swabbing floors at night.
"It was Hopkins I followed first," he muttered. "Then Baudelaire.
And as the light frizzled in my brain, I brought Commies to the light

at Yaddo, then found myself confined like Ezra Pound. How clear
things were, then weren't. Then one more twist
rounding Skull Hill and Hell's skunk hour slouching near.

I was a Lowell, and answered the President as an equal. The list
goes on, recorded in sonnet sonnet sonnet as history
groundhogged itself again and then again. My wives, too, quiz-

ing me in those endless hours as I tried to breathe. Oh, the sophistry
of those powerbrokers, as Ezra showed me there in his bughouse.
And when I found my boozy dolphin, I sang once more the mystery

of it all. Then the ending in a taxi as I headed back to Lizzie, spouse
two as my heart gave out. *Sauve qui peut,* they shouted, as the men
broke and fled. *Save yourself, if you can.* Be quiet, little mouse.

There, be quiet, now." And with that he drifted off, as when
a candle smolders, then goes dark. "He did nobly, Cal did. Did
what he could." It was a young man's voice this time. "Again

and again, he tried to revive himself in his revising," it said.
I looked up to make out the broken face of Crane, the Heart,
who sang of love and Liberty and the Brooklyn Bridge, dead

now these ninety years. "It was my love for a sailor at the start
that led to each failed voyage, then on and on to her. At last,
having failed to make a sailor down below, I made a fresh start

by exiting my cabin and heading to the stern that noon, then cast
my gaze down into the vast Atlantic, then waved adieux
and jumped. Ah, the faces staring from their deckchairs, aghast

as I let go, wed finally to the sea, which keeps me now
forever and for good." "Still, you sing among the spheres,"
I gasped. "You, our Chaplin, our weeping clown, our own Pierrot.

How many dawns, chill from your rippling rest. . . . The tears,
the jeers, the fears, the cares, the too few years you had.
You, hand in hand with that other Brooklyn bard those years

before, as he gazed from the ferry's prow at that big bad
city. Praise for all those blessed songs you had to offer.
You, who sang our New World rivers, so promising. . .and sad."

Then, as he too drifted back into the dark to sing and suffer
that fevered vision of his broken tower, I heard a voice
grow clearer, as syllables coalesced now into ideas of order.

"A mind of winter," he sighed, "as if one ever had a choice.
Or thirteen ways of wording a world of multifoliate inflection,
a mundo of gay waltzes where for a moment we rejoice,

before the band stops playing and all becomes dejection
or blank rejection. Still, the world cries out, 'Let there be light,'
even when you've lost your perfect wife. Still, the imagination

hungers for that final rendezvous, some shawl for warmth, as night
comes on and blackbirds hover overhead and we leave our work
and head blind for home, each step tap-tapping to get the music right."

And now, my time here over, I glimpsed the Doc, the stark
dignity of his entrance after all this time come to tell me what
I'd hoped for. "Yes," he smiled, "a change will come to mark

the nature of our lines and vivify for those who from the start
sought words rooted in a place and a music to define their art
and leave it etched there on the mind. And, even better, on the heart."

REMEMBERING PHIL LEVINE

There were times when it seemed to me even you
could almost believe something out there was waiting.
Something you called massive, irrational, yet so
powerful even the mountains had no word for it.

No, you weren't crazy, as you liked to say. Sly, yes,
as always, but far from crazy. How often you had me
laughing so hard I had to beg you (to no avail, of course)
to please stop so I could catch my breath again.

But then, Phil, that was you. How lucky to know you,
from when we taught together up at Bread Loaf those
late summers, you talking about your brilliant teacher, John
Berryman. Or you up at the lectern, your words like lightning

as you recalled those years hauling furniture up flights
of rickety stairs for some old couple, or working those
punch presses in Detroit. Or those years teaching at Fresno,
where you transformed the lives of so many students.

Or the two of us strolling through that SoHo gallery with those
black and white photos of Spain's anarchists your friends
fought alongside back then, some never coming back home.
Your words for Ascaso, a man of stone resting now among those stones.

Or those long talks when you taught down in New York, living in that
high rise Village apartment with Franny, you reciting "Do Not Go
Gentle into That Good Night," the whole poem by heart,
in a way that could turn even an agnostic into a believer.

Or your time on Brooklyn's Willow Street, as we strolled south
along the darkening East River, and I kept recalling that
tenement and first home up on East 51st. Still, this was Hart
Crane's world, the one he transformed from gray grit

into a paradise I could almost believe in, as we gazed on
Lady Liberty and the Brooklyn Bridge and dusk descended
that autumn night and you stopped a couple of young
Brits and asked them to take a picture of the two of us.

Or that last meal we had together with dear Franny
at some Polish restaurant you both loved a few blocks over.
Then, as we finished, me saying it was time to get the bill
and you saying, no, it was time for *me* to get the bill.

Then the three of us walking to the subway under
the streetlights as I headed back into Manhattan that night,
you jabbing me with those one-liners, and you grabbed
my arm, as if this might well be our last time together.

And then that final call to Fresno as Franny held the phone
to your ear, you trying to joke, and my one good ear failing
me again, so that I couldn't make out your words, and whispered
goodbye, as now I wait to laugh with you across that great divide.

SEPARATED BY 2477 MILES, I LAUGH
WITH BOB PACK OVER THE PHONE

"So Moses comes down from Mount Sinai," Bob begins
again, his voice relaxed, but as ready as Bach to pack
a whammy. It's something fifty years of forth and back
and forth have taught me, a way of paying for my sins.

"So he comes running down the mountain, headed for
this circle of elders by some fire pit waiting for whatever news
he has for them. 'Well, we had some time to get to schmooze
up there,' he sez. 'And I got good news and some bad to share.

The good news first. I haggled the Commandments down
to ten.'" And I'm already laughing, as Bob waits, then kicks
in with, "'The bad news is that thing about adultery still sticks.'"
And then I'm laughing so hard I'm drowning in my own

guffaws and he knows he's got me once again. And just
so you really understand how Bob's tortured me with jokes
all these years, there's the one about the wife who provokes
her sick husband into seeing their specialist to discuss

what's wrong with him. So the doc takes the husband
inside and gives him a thorough examination, only to walk
him back outside and ask the man's wife if they can talk.
Then he tells her hubby will need some very special attention.

"He's depressed. His life's just ebbing," she hears the doc sigh.
"But you could help him by greeting him at the door each night
with a sexy nightgown on, then cook a special dinner for his delight.
And when hubby asks what went on, she says, "'You're gonna die.'"

Multiply such delicious jokes a hundredfold and you get the point.
Sure, we've had a many serious talk as well, back in the day,
at his home or mine, or up in Frost's cabin in that Bread Loaf phase,
when we were younger and poured out poems to rock the joint.

"And though we're bonded here on earth," you wrote,
"we see our laughing selves floating up, beyond all ache,
where we will grieve no more about such loss." So, let's take
away from all of this elegiac stuff our laughter, that high note

that will last long after we're both gone, dear friend, like those
paired trombones you hear reverberating in those purple hills
you have sung so often of, or those loon calls and ebbing trills
of airy laughter as on and on like two rabbis our blessèd banter flows.

EMILY WAVES FROM HER BEDROOM WINDOW AS WE PASS BY

The drumbeat of your church hymn form
Your four threes four threes riffling on.
Those Ghosts beneath your evergreens
Gathering as the Sun goes down—

I felt a Funeral, in my Brain,
You sighed, full knowing well
What with the deaths of A and B
That soon the Bell would have to knell

For you as well across the Land
Of Goldenrod and Rose
As now those Gentian flocks perk up
And tilt their Parasols

And Shadows gather once again
Across that open field—
All headed for the burial Ground
Where Secrets must stay sealed

Yes, once again we mourn your loss
As now we follow after—
Hoping to learn as time treads on
The courage of your laughter

THE OTHER SIDE

All those years you lunched with Margaret, or spent time
cooking meals together, baking cookies, batch after batch.
Meals at Thanksgiving and, yes, especially come Christmastime.

Our boys out on the lawn beneath the maples playing catch.
Oh, those years vacationing on the Cape or strolling the avenues
of Naples and ancient Pompey with its new uncovered news.

And now here we were beside her as the end drew near,
this lovely woman we'd known for over fifty years,
her body wracked with illness after illness and so much pain.

There was her younger son, who'd flown in from Eugene
with his wife and kids to comfort her now, his guitar
strumming an old ballad about going home at last.

Her other boy was missing, no longer there for her,
and there was nothing we could do to change that now.
And there was Jim, lost in that dark moment, trying to find

something in images of Roman cemeteries, his mind
grasping for whatever Seneca or Cicero might tell him now.
Still, what did the future hold for him? The past was past.

That much we understood, as on each fleeting moment fled.
But then there you were, my dear, kneeling down beside
her as she sat hunched, staring helplessly on her bed

as suddenly you gazed into her near-vacant eyes and said,
"We'll lunch again together, Margaret, on the other side,"
the words surprising us, until stoic Jim let go at last and cried.

And so it goes. The unanswered questions you dare not ask.
And then the moment that undoes death's dreaded mask.
Yes, dear Margaret, we'll lunch together on the other side.

AND NOW

they tell me, compañero, that you're leaving,
after all these years your time come round at last.
Forty years, forty years since that cold spring weekend
with our brother Cursillistas down in Holyoke.
Fifty men and more there in that chapel, when
we learned the news that death was closing in.

And there you were, my friend, as if just yesterday,
standing upright in that circle next to me,
your voice rising before I heard it crack, as on
we sang "How Great Thou Art." Ah, those words!
Those words that caught me by surprise, though
I have sung the song five hundred times and more.

My eyes kept moving up to look upon the crucifix,
Christ's head bent forward to say his work was done.
And when I think, we sang, *that God, His Son not sparing*
Sent Him to die, I scarce can take it in
That on the Cross, my burden gladly bearing
He bled and died to take away my sin. . . .

And yet she too was praying. Yes, your dear Maria,
ella oró con todo su corazón, ah, with all her heart,
for you had told me, braced like the soldier you'd been
years before there on North Korea's hellish frozen hills,
that no—no!—she was not about to let you go this time.
And, Lenny, here's the thing, after we'd all returned

to the warmth and comfort of our homes, we learned
the stunning news that somehow, Lazarus-like,
you had returned to health and life and would go on
for another forty years. This I cannot explain, my friend,
nor in truth do I even dare, but can only marvel at the fact,
and give the Lord and your dear Maria my heartfelt thanks.

And now that the end has come round at last, and your
loved ones have gathered round you, can you hear it?
Can you hear the music as he calls out to you, this time to take
you home? Can you feel that inexplicable joy, *amigo mio*,
as you gaze, as I pray I too will, in humble adoration, our words
calling out again and then again, "My God, how great Thou art!"

Leonardo Rodriguez (1928–2021)

THE CALL

Caravaggio, *The Calling of St. Matthew*, 1599-1600.

Like God the Father in Michelangelo's Sistine Chapel
who searches Adam's face, stretching his right arm
out to touch and awaken him to life, so here
in Caravaggio's painting above the altar of King
Louis there in Rome, it is Jesus this time round reaching

out his arm toward the tax collector Matthew, who
in turn points his own hand toward himself, stunned
at being singled out like this. In the meantime, two
young tax collectors, startled as if they too have been
uncovered, look up for an instant, while another two,

one who's clearly been in the money-laundering
business a long time now, keep their heads down,
preoccupied with the pile of silver coins aglitter there
on the coarse-grained table half hidden in the shadows.
The preternatural light—let's call it that—that struggles

with the dark seems to catch the drama of it all: a gift
offered in that instant that could satisfy a hungry heart.
And—look!—there's Christ's hand held out again, ten years
on, Caravaggio pointing out the truth again, as the dead man
Lazarus is jolted back once more into the light, his arms flailing

as life begins to flow back into his limbs. He was a brawler,
no doubt, this Caravaggio. And just how many he maimed
or killed or conned must be left for scholars to figure out.
But a many few at least. First he fled Milan, then Rome,
then in time it was on to Naples. Then on again, this time

to seek protection from those Knights in Malta. Then
finally it was down to Sicily, before he headed back to Rome,
sailing up the coast, hoping once again to be pardoned,
this time by no less than the pope himself, in exchange of course
for those final priceless paintings only Caravaggio

himself could execute. Among the three there's one
of Saint Ursula at the very instant the mad Hun's
arrow penetrates her breast, as now she gazes down
at what's just happened, her eyes those of a contemplative,
accepting of the end she's reached, while the artist,

who surely knew his share of sharps and gangsters,
reveals himself as one more member of the gang, staring
down now in disbelief at what his brushstrokes have revealed
about himself, even as the scene screams before his eyes.
Brother, sister, he was much like one of us, I fear.

Someone no doubt who felt unworthy to be singled out,
yet someone who could paint far better than his rivals, as well
he knew himself. Someone too who saw deeper than most
of us, as his paintings likewise clearly show. Yes, there was a price
upon his head, for sure. But how much only God can know.

NEWS THAT STAYS NEWS

Thirty years back, an old friend, the poet Bill Matthews,
told me something over a drink that still sticks with me.
Something his father had once told him: that the best way to read
the world's ever-constant troubles was to let the whole mess

go. So, when you glance at the morning news, he said, or hear
some bad news on the radio, some catastrophe that catches
your attention for the moment, the way a louse latches
onto your arm or leg, think of some metaphysical dog, aware

once more of some noisome itch, who rouses to raise its paw
to squelch the damn thing, before the hound plops its head down
once again and goes back to sleep. That is, until the next round
of itching sets him off again. Take that tsunami that saw

all those atomic reactors on Japan's coast melt down, unleash-
ing one hell of a chain reaction. Or the eight point earthquake
burying towns down there in Brazil, bodies sinking in the wake
of a riverine avalanche of indifferent mud. Or those cease-

less fires way down under in Australia. Or, closer, there in California.
Or even closer now, where some neighbor up in our Vermont hills
has invited one and all to come on over and test their killing skills
on his firing range with its horde of AK-47s meant to warn

aspiring patriots of the need to make Amurka great again.
But what's the news that stays news every day? And where
shall we look to find it? Consider those outlier pilgrims, aware
that Philip—given his Greek name—could ask the Man to explain

what He was doing there in the temple precinct now. Was he
the one, the Messiah, and—if so—what did a moniker like that mean?
Recall this was Passover, deliverance time in a way still unforeseen.
Still, now, Christ told them, the hour'd come for the Son of Man to be

glorified. But what did that mean either? they tried to puzzle through.
Death—his own death—was what he was speaking of. How a grain
of wheat must first die to itself so that it can at last rise again
transformed to multiply a billion billionfold. A breakthrough

like no other, where death would not only go back to sleep but die.
Still, for that to happen He would have to undergo the bitter taste
of death, but first betrayal by his closest friends, only to be debased
and spat upon, then whipped and led out to the Skull and crucified.

In the meantime, there were other questions demanding answers before
these righteous folk would be willing at least fifty-fifty to sign on.
Like: just who was this Son of Man he spoke of? And on and on and on.
Well, he'd be gone soon enough, his work here done. And much more

pressing: his victory over that ancient leering serpent still coiling
itself around the entire human race, still intent on squeezing the very life
from us. For *this* was why he'd come: to end our age-old strife
and let the Good News easter in each one of us in the rising of the King.

THE WHEEL, THE WHEEL. . .

Sixteen and a half with a brand new driver's
license in my wallet, driving my father's
'47 two-toned old clunky Pontiac,
I turned left off Hempstead Turnpike, when a
car (what make or color I can't recall) appears
shark-like off to my right and it's there
in front of me and I'm twisting the steering
wheel first left then right when somehow—
and this I swear to, friend—the wheel itself
takes over, spinning this way then that
the danger's past and the car disappears
into the past, and I breathe again. This was
sixty-five years ago, mind you, and still
I can't explain what happened.

Do you believe in Guardian Angels?
Well, since that day I confess I do. I don't know
if they have wings or not, but they sure
have strength, like the one who wrestled
Jacob that dark night. And they're there, all right.

The wheel, the wheel. That Force behind
those starry wheels that spin about the earth.
Heaven wheels above you, revealing her great glories,
Dante sang, *and still your eyes stay focused
on the ground.* But trapped behind that wheel,
something deigned to save the car and me,
and I alone am left to tell the story.

SUPPER AT EMMAUS

Caravaggio, *Supper at Emmaus*, 1605-06.

And there's that hand again, reaching out this time
to bless the bread that's been set before him on the table.
It's a small loaf, really, just a roll, and it's been broken,
much as his body was three days before. To his left
there's a pewter pitcher with black lines striped across
it and a glass half hidden, filled with bloodred wine.

He must be real, this Nazarene, because you can see
his shadow on the worn leather jacket the old innkeeper's
wearing, who's gazing down at this stranger as he wonders
what's going on. In the foreground, seated, are two disciples:
one is Cleophas, the other, strangely, looks like Peter, at least
from other portraits Caravaggio painted of the man.

The same disciple who denied Christ three times out there
in the courtyard, and who now seems to inch his right hand
close and closer to Christ's wrist, as if to check if this could
really be the Man. In the upper right stands an old woman,
bent and weary from the daily chores she's done so long
that nothing seems to faze her anymore, so that as the Man

breaks bread as an offering of himself, we cannot read
what it is she's thinking. And here's the thing: there's another
version of this same scene, which Caravaggio painted
five years earlier. In this one Christ appears clean-shaven
and is so much younger, which may be why the men failed
at first to recognize this stranger who had walked beside them.

But look at what the painter's rendered. There's a glass carafe
of wine, a bowl of fruit and a roasted capon on the table, a Sunday
feast for sure. And once again an innkeeper stands looking down,
puzzled as this stranger blesses the bread then breaks it, even
as those two disciples are clearly shaken—perhaps like us
as well—by what is really happening here before our eyes.

Acknowledgments

The following poems first appeared in the following publications, for which my heartfelt thanks.

America
First Things
Image
Italian Americana
McMaster Journal of Theology and Ministry
Montague Reporter
North American Review
Paterson Literary Review
Poems from Pandemia, ed. Patrick Cotter, Southword Editions: The Munster Literature Centre, 2020.
Smartish Pace
Valley Voices: A Literary Review

This book was set in Perpetua, designed by the British sculptor, artist, and typographer Eric Gill, in response to a commission in 1925 from Stanley Morrison, an influential historian of typography and adviser to the Monotype foundry. The design for Perpetua grew out of Gill's experience as a stonecarver and the name pays tribute to the early Christian martyr Vibia Perpetua.

This book was designed by Shannon Carter, Ian Creeger, and Gregory Wolfe and proofread by Sharon Mollerus. It was published in hardcover, paperback, and electronic formats by Slant Books, Seattle, Washington.

Cover art: Alfonse Borysewicz, *Mustard Seed*, 2022.

www.ingramcontent.com/pod-product-compliance
Lightning Source LLC
LaVergne TN
LVHW090039090426
835510LV00038B/898